# BORROWED WAVE

*Rachel Moritz*

KORE PRESS   TUCSON   2015

Kore Press, Inc., Tucson, Arizona USA
*Standing by women's words since 1993*
www.korepress.org

Copyright© 2015 Rachel Moritz

All rights reserved. No part of this book may be used or reproduced in any manner whatsoever without written permission from the publisher except in the case of brief quotations in critical articles and reviews.

Design and composition by Sally Geier

We express gratitude for individual gifts and for support from the National Endowment for the Arts which, in part, has made this Kore Press publication possible.

ISBN: 978-1-888553-67-3
Library of Congress Cataloging-in-Publication Data

Moritz, Rachel.
  [Poems. Selections]
  Borrowed Wave / Rachel Moritz.
     pages cm
  Includes bibliographical references.
  ISBN 978-1-888553-67-3 -- ISBN 1-888553-67-7
  I. Title.
  PS3613.O7544A6 2015
  811'.6--dc23
                    2015006757

# BORROWED WAVE

CONTENTS
    Empathic Outline    1

ONE
    Borrowed Wave    5
    Nascency    9
    Little House    10
    Itinerant    11
    Island of    14
    Animate Song    16
    Lantau Song    21

TWO
    The shape of the body; the movement and the wave-form    31
    Many forms in water may also be found in clouds    32
    The previous experiment created an abundance of new forms    33
    Approaching storm; mackerel clouds    34
    The finished forms in the sand record movement that has ceased    35
    Flowing water encounters a widely submerged obstacle    36
    Streams of air meeting at various angles    37
    A suitable duration of exposure    38
    Bell-shaped forms, which travel along with the current    39
    Between still and moving water    40
    On the spiritual nature of air    41
    Mackerel clouds in reverse    42

THREE
    Pineal    47
    Pilot    50
    Strange Beauty    51
    Assembly Notes    52

Song with Peacock    56

Real Curvature    57

Kind Song    58

Homozygous    60

Boundary Surface    63

Sumac    64

*Notes*    67

*Acknowledgments*    69

*But internal difference,*
*Where the Meanings, are—*

EMILY DICKINSON

EMPATHIC OUTLINE

Branches of the pine trees sway in this other season

like our apartment in the seventies, back and forth, typhoon—

Grapevines wearing cardboard shields, diagonal across a field

The streak of storm cloud signals rain

Distantly, thought has divorced feeling

without papers, no possible remarrying—

'Icy,' says the street, announcing its future

Apple trees with lichen as second bark on this road

The wizened fruit hangs, appears to speak before I try

So you can believe in the past, but it is still deciding

Imagine the vineyard, men digging

with shirts around their waists

—Emotion hovers, her own soloist

# ONE

## BORROWED WAVE

(In childhood, a caught space)


Your Nana was ironing sheets
    in her Lemon Joy kitchen.

Wings without body, linen snagged on the lip
    of her board. Was she a bird?

'I can smell the rubbers in the front entry
    as I sat on the hall-tree seat and hunted
    for my galoshes,' she wrote,

remembering how an object locates—

You were drinking milk from her blue Delft teacup. By the slice of window you lifted up
    her teacup, left a rim of white on blue flowers.

Little moths or butterflies, parting waves.

'A sudden brightness of white
    tablecloth on the big round table in the dining room'

tea + cup (deft granddaughter forms a thing
    in her mind)

but the wave of nostalgia is borrowed. You remember
    sleeping beneath a moss-green scroll whose scholars
    bent the footbridge in a Taoist garden.

'Click of rug guards on the stairs as I tip-toe down'

And something caught in the rim of your throat
    when her shadow slipped over concrete. Sprinklers
    pulsed the cemetery, fireflies, cracks in sidewalk
    her sandals barely missed.

(Also about spatial memory, as if screened)


Lost in the scroll, like vision, is her breath beneath
    a rose-colored comforter when you peer in
    the bedroom. Her bed with its polished cherry
    headboard. Mostly, Nana breathes with eyes shut.

 'the shine on Mother's circular china closet'

One night, a motorcyclist hits their meridian. After a terrible
    screech, neighbors pile the sidewalk. The ambulance sirens.
    You remember a blast of after-rain steam against your
    nightgown, which inside the condominium, beneath
    the moss scroll, has felt very cool in the hum.

Someone pounds their front door,
    wakes you—

In the morning, his boot sits
    straight up beneath her Oldsmobile,

leather tongue splayed
    like a monkey cup plant.


She opens the car door slowly, as if

    connecting dots.

(And ideas about scaffolding and foreground)

The window bars straight down, their iron parallel.

You were visiting America, where the guest room
    window attached to your dream.

Someone searing the bars and reaching—

Your head was by wall and your feet by window.
    Outside a steel mobile glinted at night in the carport,
    headlights streaked the walls, the Taoist backs crossing
    the footbridge, three panes of fabric from a dark wooden rod.

In art, another country continued inside
    time, people on a planked bridge with swallows.

Dusk losing edges.

She keeps coming in to speak you to sleep.

Sleep tight. Sleep tight. Repeat
    three times for each bar on the window.

The scholars go on playing cards.

Over there, remembering bamboo
    bent around the buildings.

Sleep, tight.


(Opening the door, a wildness in the lip of her galoshes)

## NASCENCY
### HONG KONG 1977

Nomadic, our figure of shoreline roams

Of elbowed sand and island's intimate salt

Of alleyways colonial in their dingy whites,

the doorways tin strips

budgies craft from daylight

How long have you lived, asks the world

as we arrive in it, twinned rooms

salient with mosquito netting, sheets

in a hallway's silk profusion

And lauded, our missing drifts—

through each of four walls

walks the relapse of relic

Just as I'm following you, animate pause

## LITTLE HOUSE

1. This way of being inside a parent's necessity.

2. Up at night, leaned on the whitewashed walls, several variations to pain.

3. Not unlike our later episodes.

4. I call the animation, growing down.

5. As a great deal of wood goes loaded into a fireplace.

6. Wildly hinged, the valley's lean-to, vined by its bare boughs.

7. This way of being inside fear is childhood.

8. Anodyne, gold basilica of air.

9. The very act we responded to, locking our windows and doors.

10. Not understanding how long the house requires of you.

11. As a great deal of wood goes loaded into, sired.

**ITINERANT**
BOSTON 1983

Whatever alibi the fountain kept,
we won't discover.

      City streets grayed over

like an advent calendar
we didn't want to open,

where each speck walked across—
transient, human.


The temple dome with its lucent hello,

Christian Science sequencing
water where God

threw his light, his pool
for tossing pennies; he'd become

the tourist more now
than here.

How a cockroach flew home with us,
swollen equatorial

abiding in a moving box
by the cobra drained of blood,


and proving whatever we knew
as the past was haunted

by shape,

how distance withers.


That same glass globe we traveled
in the hushed room,

a bridge led inside
oceans, crystalline,

and each country's
name, weightless,

its blue borders.

What was familiar.

What sidewalks     grafted from Reaganite snow.


Hands bared and breath through thin walls, row house
windows bricked like strays.


Did you come from the hills
over there?

I swallowed a scrap paper written down, relative
names.


What boat keeled with bodies
'there' remained

      —the people without.

Post-Vietnam, pre-
Aquino on his airplane tarmac.


How someone was always male
when he died; someone decanting event

into death,
where time went.

## ISLAND OF

Who was waiting on the cliff when canoes arrived like buzzards

Who were you waiting for before you came

Conch shell, trying to make your voice its capacity

When I was younger all my images

got swallowed by the catch

Came bearing acorns, asked for abalone in exchange

When she sees him on the cliff with a spear in hand, she dives

off the helm of a boat into waves

no one watches her entering

Who has lost her foundation, slender

reeds against a roofline

I could never leave while I was living there but later

cormorants and otters swam close to the text

hoping for names

There is remembered place and then the place you are leaving

In the shallow bay, trees covering themselves with kelp

are sleeping

## ANIMATE SONG

I'd believe the past is fragment,

but for its narrow intimation of a door,

and the house waiting, all stucco and wet

where hummingbirds catch still

inside our kitchen tiles, and time

has no shape, in stasis;

prismatic whites dot the harbor

like vertebrae

gathering forms of rain

In the form of my absence left long enough,

two saviors disguised as parents

ride in where life begins

Twinned above their bedspread,

pillows sleep like dormant waves

Where was my body when before

hadn't vanished?

As the logic of children is nearest

the logic of gods; staring into eyes of the dead

as if I knew them

As if I knew the indiscretions of memory,

could they be my mind

developing its rooms?

Our floor in wooden squares led backwards

through the house, curved rattan

and metal windowsills, breakers for typhoon

As if someone punctures a hole in my throat,

and the puppet mouth rises

Wind squalling past the other country

Hear a little why

of bamboo

Hear the wind squalling past trees

on a curved surface, though life has its shape

we can't conceive

And where the window won't dispense

with time, each night is

a small good-bye; the child

passenger rides with fear

Thoughts blown—her vast body

barely arrived, it seems half over

Each decade a gate you unlatch

and crawl inside, until the last,

already knowing you, that waits

Already knowing the artifice of dream,

our doorway carves open water

where I wait, fire ants chafing my ankles

As when you leave a presence,

a presence disappears

Sails wipe back

Junks dissolve in the harbor

I imagine myself a traveler with taut stick and rag

carried on my back,

some long telegraphy

## LANTAU SONG

The sea elastic with sun

The little boats slung over

sand and waves breaking

on pilings covered with shell

We once rode past an island

neither real nor inhabited

dream. I knew the color was

this color. At the peak of hillside

a woman stood carved and facing

wind. She was known to protect

sailors we climbed her many stairs

the air humid I hardly breathed

There was yet more invisible landscape

to learn to see

Dear small palm tree in island

fog or island of wild cats and

bricks blood-colored

Some of the fruit was named for stars

and tasted bitter

A palm leaf holds water

A palm leads down

the hillside into ruin

There was something about the glide

of houses on stilts, thatched roofs

of reeds and tile. At night the hills

rose around us in the dark I felt

I was home after some long time away

You said the poem was language held as glass

to light coming through a window

What radiates rather than tells

The past feels this way becomes

invisible becomes landscape

On a path through trees were the cabins

covered in mist so thick we couldn't see

them but touched the edge of stone

wall and knew it was that place

What is nostalgia good for if not

to remember an idea you wanted

Ovaltine in tin mugs the morning's

tenor kept being taken away

from places I felt joy in

A cable car riding coastline

where we lived I was sad but not

unhappy felt more like regaining what was mine

had stayed alive there

what did it mean

Green façade where hills descend

a sunset over water

We hiked the stairs by the side of the beach

and tried to find a rock formation

in the photograph. If I say

I am no longer suspicious

of joy will you believe me

There was something about finding sun

where steeped the harbor overdone

with wealth and painted colors

the buildings no longer full of mold

Still I want to end with some description

of water which was always when I dreamed

an inventory waiting

where I didn't know

or some invisible landscape learning

to radiate where it remained

TWO

*Like water, thought can create forms, can unite and relate the forms to one another as ideas; it can unite, but also separate and analyse. The capacity of water in the realm of substance to dissolve and bind together reappears in thinking as a spiritual activity.*

THEODOR SCHWENK

## THE SHAPE OF ITS BODY, THE MOVEMENT AND THE WAVEFORM

I left her in the kitchen, with a woman older than myself.

'She'll make a better mother,'
I knew such weight wasn't finite.

The car purred away on gravel, and where
she remained audible,

wind might break these trees.
Dense emporium. Gap, its *not yet*—

## MANY FORMS IN WATER MAY ALSO BE FOUND IN CLOUDS

In the turning season, your one clay divided from hers. Like swans, riding a tourniquet of wind. Winter's aureole, cleft before a fallen oak whose breath is your only explanation. Whose path yields the cabin door, hard of hand on burnished leaves. And whose water gathers from the pump, the dark maker. Glued to a world your senses decided, as when millions of years earlier the silence of nature broke.

## THE PREVIOUS EXPERIMENT CREATED AN ABUNDANCE OF NEW FORMS

We were buying a white box in the ground together, and then the box strangely emptied of value. What does it mean, this spiritual failure? We'd made a woven knot on a day with halved name. The object of life, after all, is each object. How we staved off its name for bloom, not caring whether our flower was bitter.

## APPROACHING STORM; MACKEREL CLOUDS

Will you lay me down unmade as wilderness? As crows amass like arrows at our back, and the window ascends. You see, you might have said, one thing I've got a grip on is remove. The daughter of everyone and no one. Don't look at stars if you can gaze on me. Or without the idea of wilderness, this country of life remains only an idea. You have to come to the end of your concept of a human family: the body's fluids, its ribbon of heat rising past digits black in air. What does it mean to wake by a window? The terror of love—staying, and staying in place.

## THE FINISHED FORMS IN THE SAND RECORD MOVEMENT THAT HAS CEASED

I carried her through the woods, slept in waterlogged leaves
with her body on my chest. Had I known I might translate the
physical nature of love into language. My verb, desiring the noun
of her enough. Had I followed my act with a coal-black comma,
a reticent tapping on the plates of her skull, each slim erosion.
She was then my prodigal daughter, the actual without faith.

## FLOWING WATER ENCOUNTERS A WIDELY SUBMERGED OBSTACLE

As we were standing 'on' the boundary or as we were 'of' that bald lineation. Renaming our sound erupted from the lake, green as a lawn delivered holy. How, from moss-embalmed water, we dragged its wild face. On a path with both legs, synapse of boarding. How we carried the bell down irrevocable stairs, passed our sentence of doubt and kept moving.

## STREAMS OF AIR MEETING AT VARIOUS ANGLES

Little green plants held onto earth, a presence nearer than we knew or liked to imagine. As when I filmed the wild flowers up close, my hands induced their terrible shaking. My hands, leaking white on clothes pressed to my thighs. Unmade, ungathered. Just a few owned flowers and the mind's dissolution. That imagined space, I thought, while walking beyond the garden, could it be held inside me even as I shifted form?

## A SUITABLE DURATION OF EXPOSURE

The face of the child, or how I said my motherhood was only metaphoric. How it rose against our unmade hill, kept turning to look where you said there was no one. Where sumac wizened on standing branches, we were pulled, you said, or how we found phrasing. Two paths traveling parallel, media of air following like an absent man. And what is a nearness like ours if we each remain, in our own way, concealed?

## BELL-SHAPED FORMS, WHICH TRAVEL ALONG WITH THE CURRENT

And when the great moment knocks at the door of your life no louder than your heart beating, is it very easy to miss? As wind wakes the shrub roses, your battery of doubt seeding its smaller nature. The deck sways out into leaves, electric the lawn where birds skate. They want to go, I want to be with them in love with making an unknown thing.

## BETWEEN STILL AND MOVING WATER

Past the synchronous body lies an impasse of mist. Trees smoking, their bright surfaces. Past my thought about a thing, and then, splendidly, nothing of matter. How you were no longer in the woods with me but walking in my mind. And wind where you were invisible, neither weight nor smallest bearing whom, in writing herself, comes clean.

## ON THE SPIRITUAL NATURE OF AIR

I made a mark in my soul where she and I might live. Flames of air-borne will where she's audible, or do you know how to stay with strong emotion? She comes to me in dreams, tastes of salt and wants nothing but to watch. If her chance doesn't arrive for you, there's only chance to accept. I've got this body, real and failing. The soul is real, but what does she want?

## MACKEREL CLOUDS IN REVERSE

Late at night, or so in the middle. A barge with sacrificial lights electrifies the bay. As a matter of quantity, how much do you love your little question? She makes but scant breath through the windowpane, the rocks in granite circles below. How much is your emotion eating salt from their skin, lining a vaporous witness? As you can't, in your throat, either exit or digest.
I mean, returning to your question with some imprint of yes.

THREE

PINEAL

Then a cove blown taut with negatives, who is

walking the lake ions,

inland as a pane of glass
betters the world by turning

in—world,

did you rest well? Such reticence I slept

your nexus with my mouth
staved and swallowed

the shoreline or the last
leaf of year.


As if the year were a window;

a window, waking

in the gland's illumined
temple.

Pine trees, their severance.

Hare perched on shadowboxed
snow.


Carry me down this road no leaving but life-
saving the cloak bears one

and one.


A plural of pupils
counts its grammar, what is quiet

are seen things settling,

bark-stripped, leaden
wind.


Have I done some harm to the pines and you

remembering scenes

distilled without verbs?

Your shadow rails—the window

where kindness snows white.


Where branches     depth cancels
can't latch on,

mouth the tender color
of mind enough.


Maybe your joy is development.


Maybe your joy's recursive
voice could lead you

like a page leading,

blind faith.


You stand in a glass room where nothing
bad has happened.

The moon peals,    the yard tunnels
a breach into language,

hoarding its code.

## PILOT

Someone who tunnels down and away was other

My mother said, you're going where I can't be with you

As a glass idol fills its own presence with lack

and creating your light image is what counts

The stairs down into each self—how one door opened

where the man was let in

Public as flame, the self with no interior

One had no hearing for doubt in that place seen as clear

With him on the street, my spine was agent,

a world extended into, sweeping a path

Sometimes coming back in dreams, that other

kind of transparency

How our safety felt unreasonable, like I was

doing something wrong

## STRANGE BEAUTY

Morning above the reed brocade

Inside a trunk of wood by the lake

we lay, bottom feeding

and arousing few signs

Clouds phasing above

without whisper, the air jogged, didn't notice

our small quarry

Our belly, the center good ring

Purses exchanged in stunned morning

Two moats or basins, and sex is a sea

As the swan passed by our underwater

cave, came up early,

I was not witnessed by wings

blind as luminous water,

stunningly brief

## ASSEMBLY NOTES

As form holds force, a designated space,

our intimacy was the cover of two

embroiled for several years.


A married friend, 'The issues circle, but it doesn't seem
as necessary that we solve them.'


I peered within the body of our house

where a simple blue ornament,

nailed below the eaves,


made recognition of our lives
a little easier.

Would the form be our replica?

Diminutive 'we' reduced, homunculus.


I peered within the body,
saw the liver's expanse. Diffuse

human model, coil.


Just as easily as it coalesced, our marriage served
a purpose, nostalgia—


to carve away the inner

beast and leave 'okay'

on the heart.

Riding bikes across a trestle bridge in the swamp.

Birds unveiled ruby shoulders like epaulets
in the right kind of army.


I knew the female body but felt
more lost on its surface

than I cared to admit.


This 'do it yourself' love was lyric—

how could it ground to the world?


Birds with red uniforms,
calling for each other.

Or were the words now general forms
I no longer cared for?

As 'partner' carried a law firm touch.

'Wife' without 'husband.'

Our same fisted heart, the ribbed
and backwards trachea.

Structure, spoken through our bones'
wavering tent,

just as we moved closer

and visibly less.

## SONG WITH PEACOCK

Considering how a subject becomes an object without voice,

the trees bear their singular disturbance

as if they never existed apart

Their boughs together in rain-held motion, and your mind

requiring passage only thinks

the passage of time

The peacock with jeweled neck that dashes beneath branches

How you wish to feed his tentative throat your subject

without voice, his wings chalk the windows

like a residue of grief

Considering how the trees frame a subject alone in her voice

—flowering, interrupting the bird

## REAL CURVATURE

Your sense arose in me before it arose in landscape

I felt a variance inside

As if you could shine light on a field and illuminate

rain darkening the redwoods

My downward window with trees an aura nearer

than you were in the past

Before I knew my own sense of dissipation,

landscape was a line of rain and moving branches

As if the whole depth together was my own motion

rising inside the hollow bark of the tree

One motion only, a line is a wave of feeling

Who measures what's outside before she leaves

## KIND SONG

Blue-stemmed,     the boundary between us
draws itself in air

and resembles,

finally,

a highly ramified stream
shimmering in a field once

known as aversion,

or buried history.

In such form, who could have heard
our fine human memory,

our issuing voice

where the medium
recurs,     elastic over hills.

Our script, the gathered arteries.

Shared between two wild and shy animals

our pronoun,   porous
as clay

paints a whistle
over a field remaining

a field.

## HOMOZYGOUS

Barely a valley of dissimilar air

Walking, walking

Your breath visceral as

becoming is

Leaves hinged by cloud, the sunned

trunks slit open

their bark, themselves currents

in the low periphery

Valley of no one spoken for

Wrens, with their sac throats

bleating in the bush

Blossoming pupa, lost

definition

Valley of veined and recidivate branches,

of light where the wool

hangs, foundling in rain

Of water dressing soil,

a blue garment,

for when you ascend, you

are singled and ignored

Your beating apron is only

a body of upthrust

Are you a window looking in

on a window neither within

nor one of its seams, sutured wing

Paintbrush sound on the chest—*same, same*

Between each breath, the euphemed world

Now the water, ignitory,

in a state of gold duress

Wrens bathe forgiveness

in satchels of vacant air

With your lantern, your dark

wonder, you never turned down

any bravery of form

Wings of the earth-

bound inked by this pale

window who makes but little breath

Now we do with night as she does with our eyes

## BOUNDARY SURFACE

Whatever day it was. Reading/in the subway, two years younger, the metal seats shone/we tunneled across a bridge on the bronzed side not gifted for walking. /What is it about remembering, then unlocking from its fix? White buoys gather/ on the surface of the harbor, the summer cusp of rain I am traveling with her across a spatial location known as my life, and the referent is her and the past settles in water where the middle went. There is a name/to being and then un-naming. This seems to be the process of return, but more painful than building one bridge across the span of two/is knowing where it drifted. It,/as in when, /all metaphors curl their image ends like cryptic balls of yarn inhabiting/shape, perfected circles,/and what is left is the object/half, named.

## SUMAC

Confettied one, how you gladden our day.


Across the lawn it is
December, a wake blushed

where flowers once hung

illicit from their stems.


Now there is only this dilate
sun, the almond-eyed clouds the child

head renders through

as rain, left
dangling.


As many remnants of sleep
fight possibly for us,

coupling in absentia.

No one to make but ourselves.


And waves to witness
where there was none,

only driftwood.

Indelicate measures     aloneness on the shore

owned by a manger
of nothing tonguing

the skin around obvious fruit.

## NOTES

"Borrowed Wave"—Language in quotations is taken from the short story, "Easter Sunday Morning," by my grandmother, Carol Shafer.

"Itinerant"—The glass globe is the Christian Science 'Mapparium' in downtown Boston. Benigno Aquino was the exiled president of the Philippines, gunned down as he left his plane in Manila on August 21, 1983.

"Island of"—Images taken from Scott O'Dell's *Island of Blue Dolphins*.

"Lantau Song"—Lantau is an island off the coast of Hong Kong.

Titles for poems in section Two are taken from Theodor Schwenk's, *Sensitive Chaos: The Creation of Flowing Forms in Water and Air*.

"Kind Song"—Lines 10-12 borrowed from Martin Buber's *I and Thou*.

## ACKNOWLEDGMENTS

The following appeared, sometimes in different versions, in these web and print publications, with many thanks to the editors:

*26* "Island of"

*American Letters and Commentary* "The previous experiment created an abundance of new forms"

*Aufgabe* "Homozygous"

*Augury Books* online "Pilot"

*Cannibal* "Animate Song," "Strange Beauty"

*Colorado Review* "Empathic Outline"

*Counterpath* online "Pineal" (third section)

*Denver Quarterly* "Song with Peacock," "Real Curvature"

*DUSIE* "The shape of its body, the movement and the wave form"

*Free Verse* "Approaching storm; mackerel clouds," "On the spiritual nature of air," "Pineal" (first section)

*Horse Less Review* "Nascency"

*Kissed by Venus* "Assembly Notes"

*La Fovea* "Kind Song"

*Mental Contagion* "Mackerel clouds in reverse," "Between still and moving water"

*Newfound* "Itinerant"

*The Offending Adam* "Sumac," "Little House"

*TYPO* "Borrowed Wave," "Steams of air meeting at various angles"

The poems in section TWO were published as a chapbook, "Many forms in water," by above/ground press, 2014. Much gratitude to Rob Mclennan.

For support through the years, I am in debt to the teachers who encouraged me, especially Maria Damon, Deborah Keenan, and GE Patterson. I am also grateful to the Minnesota State Arts Board and the Jerome Foundation for practical support in completing this book. Thank you to all the poets in my MFA program at the University of Minnesota, who read earlier versions of this manuscript and proved such inspiring peers.

A heartfelt thanks to Elizabeth Robinson, for her generous reading, and to Brian Teare, for his words of encouragement.

To Laressa Dickey and Sun Yung Shin, much gratitude for your friendships in poetry.

Thank you, Lisa Bowden, for giving this book a chance.

Most of all, my thanks to Juliet Patterson, thoughtful reader and deft line editor, without whom nothing would be possible.

## ABOUT THE AUTHOR

Rachel Moritz received her MFA from the University of Minnesota. She is the author of five poetry chapbooks: *How Absence* (MIEL Press, 2015), *Many forms in water* (above /ground press, 2014), *Elementary Rituals* (Albion Books, 2013), *Night-Sea* (New Michigan Press, 2008), and *The Winchester Monologues* (New Michigan Press, 2005). Her poems have appeared in journals such as *American Letters and Commentary, Aufgabe, Colorado Review, Denver Quarterly, Iowa Review,* and *VOLT.*

Moritz lives with her partner and son in Minneapolis, where she publishes a poetry chaplet series from WinteRed Press and teaches creative writing in the community.

www.rachelmoritz.com

## ABOUT THE PRESS

As a community of literary activists devoted to bringing forth a diversity of women's voices through works that meet the highest artistic standards, Kore Press publishes the creative genius of women writers to deepen awareness and advance social justice.

- ° Since its inception in 1923, *Time Magazine* has had one female editor.
- ° Since 1948, the Pulitzer Prize for Fiction has gone to forty-two men and seventeen women.
- ° 26% of the members of *The New York Times* editorial board are women, 35% at *The Wall Street Journal*, and 33% at the *Los Angeles Times*.

To support feminist publishing—and help lift up "half the sky" as a way to create long-term, sustainable change and a luminous future for all—you can buy a Kore Press book directly from the publisher, make a tax-deductible gift to the vital production of contemporary women's literature, or become a member of the press at: korepress.org.